Do You Trust Me?

By

Cheryl Cunnagin

Do You Trust Me?

By

Cheryl Cunnagin

TABLE OF CONTENTS

Part II

Part III

Introduction

With great joy, I have served Jesus, praying for and ministering to many people through His name and in the power of the Holy Spirit. I stood in faith and believed Him for great and awesome things, which He has granted. Through all of this, He has twice asked me a particular question, <u>"DO YOU TRUST ME?"</u> which ultimately resulted in a major shift in my life.

Putting my trust fully in Him involved living through extremely difficult situations only God could have foreseen. That trust involved putting my faith into action, and holding on to Jesus with everything within me, no matter what the situation looked like or what I experienced. He knew what lay ahead in my life and what I needed to get through those dark places. He knows the same thing about you, too.

> "Fear not, for I have redeemed you; I have called you by your name; You are mine. When you pass through the waters, I will be

with you; And through the rivers, they shall not overflow you. When you walk through the fire, you shall not be burned. Nor shall the flame scorch you. For I am the Lord your God, the Holy One of Israel, your Savior..." Isaiah 43:1-3

PART ONE

"Weeping may endure for a night, but joy comes in the morning." Psalm 30:5

CHAPTER 1

GOD'S PLAN

God has a plan for each of us. When I discovered He created me for a plan and a purpose, it changed the way I viewed life. It has been amazing to watch His plan unfold with its various avenues and degrees. One scripture that always comes to my mind when I contemplate this is found in Ephesians 1:17-19 which reads, "that the God of our Lord Jesus Christ the Father of glory, may give to you the spirit of wisdom and revelation in the knowledge of Him, the eyes of your understanding being enlightened; that you may know what is the hope of His calling, what are the riches of the glory of His inheritance in the saints, and what is the exceeding greatness of His power toward us who believe…"

My life actually began when I accepted Jesus Christ as my Savior, and allowed Him to be the Lord of my life. I became a new creation in Him. The old things were in the past. I was forgiven. I was delivered. He filled me with His spirit and put me on His path.

He changed me from the inside out.

In a certain way, my life took its first change of direction toward Jesus when I met my husband, Ken. He brought joy to my heart. Kind and soft-spoken, he always thought of me before himself. He encouraged me to be all I could be and not settle for anything less. He was the first to ever tell me God has a plan for both of us, and he said this before we were Christians.

We met in 1980 at a police academy we were both attending. We were married in October, 1981. I knew he was the one I had waited for, the one God had for me. We completed and complemented one another. I never actually believed two people could fit together so perfectly, but somehow we did.

Ken taught me about love. Throughout my childhood, I did not feel loved or appreciated, so the rejection caused me to be distant, looking out only for the things that pertained to me. Seeing through it all, Ken was patient, gentle, and loving. When I was down, he made me laugh. When I cried, he comforted me. When I laughed, he laughed with me. When I was quiet, he left me to my thoughts. When I talked, he listened, sometimes for hours.

He always brought me flowers, most of the time without any special occasion or prompting. They ranged from simple to elegant. Once I jokingly accused him of picking them off the side of the road, and he just smiled. It was his special way of letting me know he loved me unconditionally.

When our daughters, Ami and Sara, were born several years later, Ken was the first one to hold them. He looked at them with such love. He was overjoyed with being a father of daughters because I think he knew they would grow up to be "daddy's girls."

His first daughter, Jami, from a previous marriage, was also his delight. Once, while he was lost in his thoughts, he spoke aloud, "God sure knew what he was doing when he gave me all girls!" Years later, his girls would say of Ken that he was a "girl dad" because he knew exactly how to treat them and love them.

Without realizing it, Ken was a large part of God's plan for my life. Marrying him was definitely a pivotal point. Without his gentle approach to our relationship, I certainly would have been a different person.

Our children, Jami, Ami, and Sara were God's gifts to us and very much a part of His plan as well. They brought such joy into our lives. I can't begin to explain how God used them to teach me many lessons about life, love, and faith in order to change me. He always told me to listen to them because they had such wisdom from Him. Sometimes it was a humbling experience because their insight into God's heart was more than I could grasp at a particular time.

God's "family plan" has been a significant part of His purpose for my life. The closeness and love of my family has changed me. All the lessons I have learned and experiences I have gone through prepared me to be able to minister to others on a more personal level, with God's love. I am grateful to God for His plan in my life and His wisdom to know exactly how to carry it out.

CHAPTER 2

THE WAKE UP

Married for seven years, Ken and I were thrilled to be expecting our fourth child, who would be our first son. Ken cherished each of our daughters, but also delighted in the thought of a son. An ultrasound confirmed that it was indeed a boy, and Ken wanted him named after him and his father. He would be called Kenneth L. Cunnagin III (Casey, for short).

Four and a half months pregnant, and fascinated by the life God placed within me, it was exciting to feel the baby's movements. My thoughts always drifted to what this little one would look like, and what he would grow up to be. I wondered how God would use him in His plan for his life, and I dedicated him to the Lord before he was ever born (as I did with each of my children).

I had always wanted children. It was one desire of my heart from as far back as I could remember, so I know God granted me each one. Our oldest, Jami, was Ken's daughter from a previous marriage who came to live with us. She was the artist and the helper. Ami, the observant and compassionate one, loved babies and wanted a brother. Sara, the dancer, animal lover, and creative one enjoyed watching the animal shows on television.

My priorities included being a wife, mother, and homemaker (not necessarily always in that order). On certain days, it was difficult to balance everything out with any normality. As most mothers know, life can certainly be a little chaotic most of the time! There was little refuge for me to collect my thoughts or find that rare moment of silence and calm. However, in the evening, I would sing my little ones to sleep with songs of praise to the Lord, feeling His presence envelop us, and our home filling with His peace.

My one "escape" for the week was a prayer meeting in the evening at Ruth's house. She was an elderly woman from church who loved the Lord and wanted to see God do great things in the earth. I was the youngest person in the group, but no one seemed to mind. We were all there to spend time in the Lord's presence and to do His work through prayer. Praying with people who had walked with Jesus for many years was truly a blessing to me. I learned a great deal about listening to and being sensitive to the Holy Spirit, praying things through, the power of God's Word, obedience, submission, faith, trusting Him, and being open to His plan.

At one of the prayer meetings during my third month of pregnancy, the Holy Spirit directed several people to pray for me. As they began to pray, He revealed to us the child I was carrying was a boy (this was before any ultrasound or medical confirmation), and his name would be called Judah (which means praise). I thought this a little strange since Ken had already determined to name the baby after him if he were a boy. The prayer also stated that because of this child, praise would come forth from my heart, and people would come to know Jesus because of him. I cannot express the feeling of joy that I felt at that moment.

Several months had passed since that prayer. Ken, who was a police officer, had to go to a training course for a week in a town several hours away. It was always lonely without him around, but we were use to this type of life. It was still difficult to be the lone parent in his absence.

One particular evening, after making sure the children were asleep, I attempted to read my Bible and pray only to drift off to sleep in utter exhaustion from the day's activities. Around one o'clock in the morning, the Holy Spirit woke me up to pray. I didn't know what I was praying about, as I began to pray in the spirit, but I knew whatever it was, it wasn't a good situation. I began to weep from the innermost part of my being, like I had never done before. This continued for several hours, then it was finished and the burden lifted. I sat in silence for a little while longer, wondering for whom or what the prayer was intended, but then, I fell soundly asleep.

The following evening, the same situation occurred. I prayed and wept for several hours, grieved in my soul. I had a feeling this was something close to me, but I didn't have the understanding of what it could possibly be. Perhaps it involved Ken, the children, or someone else dear to me. I continued to pray, still without a revelation. When it was finished, I again fell back to sleep.

On the third night, I began to feel such a heaviness come upon me. I didn't pray. All I could do was weep uncontrollably because I suddenly knew this was about the baby I carried. I knew somehow something was terribly wrong. Suddenly, I heard the Lord speak to me saying, "Cheryl, do you trust Me?" I was startled! *"Why would He ask me a question like that?"* I knew the answer I gave Him would somehow affect the outcome of my situation, so I didn't respond right away. The question weighed heavy on my mind. The silence was more than I could stand. At that point, all I could do was remember and consider all the things Jesus had done in my life. The memories began to flood my mind…

CHAPTER 3

SCARED TO LIFE

I remember vividly how I came to know Jesus as my Savior and Lord. I was a city police officer in a college town. It was a hot, August day, with not much activity in town since the college was in summer session. I was bored of patrolling around in the car, so I took my break. I went to the local bookstore in order to buy something to read. When I put my hand on the doorknob to open the door, I immediately found myself standing in the back of the store in front of the "religious" book section. *"How did I get to the rear of the store? I don't even remember walking in the door."* I tried to retrace my steps, but I did not remember physically walking into the bookstore. Then, I began to think something was terribly the matter with me, like I was losing my mind!

Working through the awkward feelings I had, I found a book about the end times and purchased it.

Having gone to church while growing up, I realized I had never read the Bible, let alone Revelation. The fact was, I believed in God, but never spent much time with Him other than going to church, and then only because I had to. When I prayed, I just hoped He heard me, and that He didn't have someone else's prayer to answer at the same time as mine. I was miserable with the way my life had gone (except for marrying Ken), and I didn't think God cared that much for me to change things or to make a difference.

As I drove to the local cemetery with my book (it was the only place where there was peace and quiet to read), I was still trying to figure out what had just happened to me at the bookstore. Nothing like that had ever happened to me before. *"Maybe I'm in the early stages of Alzheimer's disease...WHAT! I'm only twenty-eight years old. Maybe my brain skipped a beat, or it was something I had eaten, or maybe I didn't get enough sleep, or I am working too hard or..."* My thoughts continued to ramble on.

My eyes pondered over the book's cover, and I decided to just start reading. It's not like I would be out much anyway. I was certainly not prepared for what was about to happen. This book became alive to me. As the author guided me through a scenario of the Book of Revelation, I remembered thinking, "Why have I never read or known this before?" Fear gripped my very soul. To think that I was living in the beginning stages of all the destruction that will soon come upon the earth before Jesus' return was more than I could process. I didn't want to think about what I was reading, but for some reason, I couldn't stop reading. The message frightened me. Somehow, in my heart, I knew that this was true (not necessarily the scenario, but the book of Revelation). *"Why had I never heard about this before now?"*

My break was over, but the fear in my heart was ever present. I drove around thinking about the few chapters I was able to read and what those pages contained. *"How could this be in the Bible? How could anyone write about future events when they never live in the future? How can this be accurate? Wasn't the Bible just full of stories and history? Is God trying to tell me something? What am I missing here?"* All day long, thoughts such as these filled my head.

That evening, I continued reading through the entire book. Sleep left me. My heart raced. My head was pounding. *"What was the matter with me? If all this was true, why did I feel this way?"*

"Just throw the book away and forget it," I tried to convince myself. For a brief moment, I even considered going back to being miserable with my life rather than going on in this condition. This continued for three days!

At one point, I asked Ken if he would read the book with me, but he replied, "No, I'm not reading THAT book!" He didn't offer any other explanation. *"Where could I turn? Was I to remain stuck in this 'twilight zone'?"*

Finally, the one comforting point the author reemphasized throughout the book was that Jesus Christ, the Son of God, came to this world because He loved us and gave His life on the cross for all those who believe. Through Him, we can have forgiveness for our sins and a new life.

I was ready for that step. I knelt on my knees in my living room and began to sob. I didn't know how to pray the prayer of salvation, but in the simplest form I could, I asked Jesus to forgive me, to be the Lord of my life, and to direct my path from that day forward. Instantly, the fear left me, the weights on my life left (I actually felt them lift off me), and I was changed. I felt His presence and received His joy and peace. I knew Jesus was real and alive. I would never be the same again. I was truly BORN AGAIN. This did not have man's fingerprints on it, only God's!

CHAPTER 4

FREE INDEED

I was brought up in a home where alcohol played a role in most everyone's life. I started drinking at a young age, first because it was the acceptable thing to do, and you were "in" if you did. The sad thing was, I made myself like alcohol because it did not have an enjoyable or desirable taste to it. By the time I was in high school, I drank to drown out the feelings of not being loved, not fitting in anywhere, the disappointments, and the sorrows which had filtered into my thoughts and heart at an early age. I thought of myself as the "black sheep" of our family.

Now that my life belonged to Jesus, I thought I would still be able to drink a little, just not as much as before. This was all I had known, never realizing there was something different the Lord had for me, and that He wanted me to walk in this new life with Him. The Holy Spirit began convicting me of the alcohol problem immediately.

It began when I started reading the Bible. I was in I Corinthians, chapter 8, when the Holy Spirit showed me I was a stumbling block (with the alcohol situation) to those who were weak — my family, Ken, and two of our dearest friends specifically. I never realized my actions as a believer could either build someone up or tear him or her down. I never wanted to cause people to stumble, but my heart and desire was to have them come to Jesus also. I prayed and asked Jesus to help me with this problem.

My first course of action was to quit on my own, but I can tell you right now that didn't happen. I was addicted — not that I had to drink continuously or even every day, but I could not get rid of this in my own power or strength because it had become a habit of my lifestyle.

I talked with Ken about quitting with me, but his answer was to go ahead without him. The problem was that God was dealing with me at this point, not Ken. I couldn't attend the Alcoholics Anonymous meetings because most of the people there were people I had arrested for DUI or other alcohol related offenses — not a good scenario. I was stuck.

Around this time, I had a dream of a demonic spirit choking the life out of me, and I knew it was related to the alcohol situation.

Late one evening at work, a fellow officer and brother in the Lord was having a discussion with me concerning smoking. I remembered how much he used to smoke, and noticed he didn't anymore. I asked him how he quit (not telling him my situation with alcohol). He told me he and his wife prayed and asked God to take the desire to smoke away from them, and He delivered them from it immediately. Bells went off in my head. Jesus was my answer.

The following evening, I knelt down in my living room and lifted up my hands to heaven. I simply asked Jesus to deliver me from alcoholism and to take the desire for it away.

Immediately, I felt the desire leave my body, and I began to cry tears of joy. I praised and thanked Jesus for a long while afterward.

He then gave me the scripture in John 8:36, "Therefore if the Son makes you free, you shall be free indeed." I was to use this truth against the devil every time he tried to sway me back into alcoholism. Believe me, I was tempted numerous times throughout the days ahead, but I stood and confessed that scripture, and He made His Word become real and effective in my situation and life. The most important thing to me was that I wanted Jesus and His life for me more than I wanted anything else.

At one point, I remember Ken asking how long I planned to quit drinking. My response to him was "Forever."

What the Holy Spirit revealed to me was also true. When I was delivered and didn't drink anymore, Ken, our two friends, and other family members began to quit as well, giving their lives also over to Jesus. I didn't have to preach to them or tell them to stop drinking. They knew Jesus had indeed delivered me and set me free. From that point on, I had to think about how my actions as a believer affected those around me. It was an important reminder to me that

I am my brother's keeper and that I am a witness for Jesus in all I do.

CHAPTER 5

GOD'S INTERVENTIONS

The devil tried to kill me through several car accidents before I was saved.

One such accident occurred in the spring of 1981 in the city where I worked. A car ran a stop sign, going air born because of the dip in the road, and landed on the driver's side top and door of my car, completely crushing the driver's side.

Seconds before impact, I cried out to God. I certainly didn't understand it at the time, but I actually felt someone pick me up and set me on the passenger seat before the car plowed into mine. The events unfolded in slow motion, but in reality, it was only a split second of time.

My life was truly spared. I stepped out of the car, my side hurting, as well as my head. The two girls from the other car appeared to have suffered minor injuries, but they were bleeding and hysterical. I made them sit down on the curb with me and tried to talk calmly to them. When the police arrived, they began to assist the girls, not realizing I was involved in the collision as well.

I remember the assisting officer finally realizing it was my car, looking at the extensive damage, and then looking back at me asking, "My God, Cheryl, are you hurt?"

I will never forget my response to that question because it was something I would have never said before the accident. My response was, "It is only by the grace of God I am alive." And so it was!

A short time later, I received a letter in the mail from the mother of the girl driving the car. She wanted to thank me for being so kind to her daughter and friend at the accident scene. She said she was a Christian and that she would be praying for me…

****

Another incident occurred on my way to work one morning. It was dark and foggy as I drove the usual back roads. I heard an audible voice behind me telling me to turn on my bright lights. I didn't respond to that voice immediately as I should have. The next moment, the voice yelled louder, "TURN YOUR BRIGHTS ON!"

When I turned my bright lights on, there was a huge horse, about the size of a Clydesdale, standing in my lane. I swerved my Jeep to the right, narrowly missing the horse, but then the car began to fishtail all over the road as I tried to recover from the quick response. Fortunately, by the absolute protection of the Lord, I managed to gain the control over the Jeep so it did not flip over or wreck. When the car came to a standstill, I looked back to see if I could see the horse, but the fog was too thick to see anything. I thanked God all the way to work and throughout the day for His protection and for sparing my life that day!

****

In August, 1988, flying home from Seattle, Washington, with my one-year-old daughter, Sara, after a visit with my sister, we landed in Chicago for our connecting flight. As we were about to board the flight, there was such an urgency to pray right then. I was stepping onto the plane when I prayed, "Father, if there is anything the matter with this plane, please don't let it take off the ground. In Jesus' name I pray." We then proceeded to find our seats and settle in.

After sitting on board for a time without taking off, people began getting restless. The flight crew would not answer any questions, only commenting that the plane was delayed. Several people from the airline came on board, looking out the windows for something. After they left, it was announced the flight was cancelled—no explanation given.

Upon entering the terminal to schedule a flight home, everyone was complaining and yelling about the cancellation of the flight. In my heart, I was praising the Lord for not allowing that plane to take off. I knew it was because of His intervention we were all safe, even if we were delayed. Later, we learned from one of the flight attendants that a large bird was sucked into one of the engines within minutes of the plane landing at the airport. The officials at the airline didn't want to risk the plane taking off before their mechanics could examine and thoroughly inspect the engine. God, knowing all things, protected everyone aboard that plane from any disaster that may have occurred.

****

Another day, Ken and I took the girls horseback riding. It was my intention to walk Sara around on the pony while he went on a short ride with Jami and Ami. For some reason, Ken told me he wanted me to go with the girls and that he would take Sara. I wasn't keen on doing that, but since he insisted, I agreed with the plan. The girl at the stables showed me which horse was mine. As I approached the horse, the Holy Spirit told me to bind up and cast out the demonic spirit that was on it. I ignored what I heard, and proceeded to mount the rather large horse. Immediately, the horse started snorting and trying to buck me off. It acted like a bucking bronco. I held on for my life, knowing if I fell off, the horse would probably stomp me to death or injure me severely.

Suddenly, I heard the Lord say, "Let go. When you hit the ground, roll away."

I was terrified to do so, but quickly asked, "Which way?" If God told me to roll, He would make sure I rolled in the right direction, otherwise I would be stomped on. I then let go, fell abruptly to the ground, and rolled out of the way of the horse's hoofs.

The stable hands ran up to control the horse, and Ken made sure I wasn't injured. I remember the words one girl blurted out, "I don't know what came over him. This horse has never acted like that before!"

That day, the Lord spared me from my ignorance of not obeying Him in the first place.

****

While at a prayer meeting at church, one woman announced the Holy Spirit wanted to show each one of us plans the enemy had against us and our families so we could pray against those plans. We all began to pray in the spirit when suddenly, I saw a vision of Ken's police cruiser. The vision then zeroed in on the back seat. I felt there was something evil or dangerous about to happen to him from that back seat area, so I began to pray against that plan until I felt the peace of God come over me. The Lord then gave me the scripture, "No weapon formed against you shall prosper" (Isaiah 54:17).

That evening, I talked to Ken and told him what happened. I cautioned him to be vigilant about checking his cruiser, especially the back seat, before and after transporting someone. I also told him we should pray Isaiah 54:17 over him every day before he went to work. He agreed.

Exactly one week later, Ken called me from work to tell me about an incident. He related the following story:

He and his partner, a rookie officer, responded to a call concerning a robbery that just occurred several blocks away. A description was given of the suspect as they were traveling to the scene of the robbery. Suddenly, Ken and his partner spotted a man matching the description. They detained him, talked with him a few minutes, and believed he was a suspect worth checking out further. The rookie officer placed the suspect in the back of the cruiser and drove to the robbed store. The woman who worked at the store was talking with another officer outside when Ken and his partner drove up. She took one look at the man in the back seat and said, "That's him. That's the man who robbed me!" Ken quickly got out of the cruiser, remembering his partner had not frisked the suspect before putting him in the back seat. He proceeded to do so. Nothing was found on his person.

However, tucked between the cushions of the back seat, there was a loaded gun, cocked, and ready to fire. The man, who had been in prison for murder, told Ken he intended to kill him and his partner as they were driving back to the store, but for some reason, he could not squeeze the trigger on the gun. He had every intention of killing them and escaping in the cruiser. He couldn't figure out why his plan didn't work.

I could hear the tension in Ken's voice, and I was concerned for him. I was also well aware that God had taken care of this incident which would have turned out in tragedy. "This is what God had us pray about," I reminded him, and he agreed. We both praised and thanked God for His mercy and protection. Ken knew God spared his life that day, and from that time forward, we always prayed Isaiah 54:17 over him as he went to work.

****

A call about a bar fight had just come in. Since I was directly across the street at the police station, I would be the first to respond. As I approached the bar, I prayed God would send the rest of the officers quickly for back up, and we wouldn't be injured. Suddenly, a large male subject appeared at the top of the steps, screaming and cursing. I knew it would be a challenge for me to arrest him in his present state. When he saw me coming, he became more agitated, focusing his attention and cursing at me. As I walked up each step, I prayed a "911" prayer asking God to hurry up and send reinforcements. Just as I was about to grab hold of the man, an arm appeared from behind me and grabbed him instead. The man flew right past me, down each step, and into the waiting cruiser by the assistance of the entire police force working that night. They had lined the steps behind me without my knowledge. It was definitely God's intervention, and I thanked Him continuously throughout the evening.

****

Late one evening I was driving home from a Bible study at a friend's home. It was an hour's drive through the country and I was tired. Suddenly, the Holy Spirit spoke to me. "Watch out for the deer ahead."

I didn't see a deer, but I turned my bright lights on and slowed down. Without warning, a large buck, ran down the hill and stopped right in the middle of my lane. It stood there for about twenty seconds and then turned around and ran back up the hill. I realized had I not been obedient to what the Holy Spirit told me, an accident could have injured or killed me. I praised the Lord all the way home!

****

CHAPTER 6

GOD'S PROVISIONS

One need I had but didn't realize at the time was that of a wonderful husband. Everyone in my family married young, and I just happened to be the one hold-out, but I had not found the one I wanted to spend the rest of my life with. I remember asking God if He had someone for me who would love me as much as I would love him. If so, I continued my prayer, please send him my way. That was the end of it, and I didn't think much about it again. One month later, I signed up for the police academy in another town.

Ken and I were the last ones to sign up, so we were both in the office completing paperwork at the same time. One box on the application asked the marital status of the applicant. I attempted to look on Ken's application, but couldn't see if he was single or married. He later told me he did the same thing.

Eventually, we learned we were the only two single people in the class, and of course, everyone was trying to get us together!

We finally went out on a date at the end of the academy, in June, 1980, due to several people nudging us on. By August, he asked me to marry him. I am glad I prayed. I will always thank God for him.

****

When I was a police officer, I had to walk uptown one evening. I came across a young man, well known in town for not being able to take proper care of himself. I asked him how he was doing, and as he began to speak, the Holy Spirit told me he had not had not eaten that day, and I was to give him the money in my pocket to get food. It was the only money I had, and I was quite hungry myself, so in all honesty, I hesitated. When I asked if he had eaten, and he said, "No, I didn't have any money." I pulled out every piece of money in my pocket and gave it to him. I told him to walk over to the restaurant across the street and get something to eat. I watched him go in, and he did.

I told the Lord I would fast the rest of the night, even though my stomach disagreed with grumbling. I continued walking around uptown, trying to think of something other than food. I began walking down an alley when the Holy Spirit told me to stop, turn right, and walk straight to the back of a building. I did so, but felt pretty silly standing there looking at the building. Then He said, "Look down." At my feet was about ten dollars in various bills and change. "Now go get something to eat," He said. What a lesson!

****

In 1984, when I was pregnant with Ami, I had a strong desire to stay at home and raise my own children. I didn't want someone else taking care of them or raising them. One day, while I was in prayer about this matter, the Lord spoke to me and told me He would grant me the desire of my heart by allowing me to stay at home with my children. I was so excited! I went to Ken and told him all that the Lord said. Ken's reaction was, "There is NO WAY you can quit your job to be at home!" WOW. I thought I must have heard the Lord wrong about this one. So I went back to prayer, and the Lord again told me the same thing. This time I didn't tell Ken. I figured we had six more months and God could surely show him in that amount of time.

Ken really wanted me to stay at home, but he was worried about the financial end of it. After all, I made more money than he did, and this would cut our finances by more than half. He just couldn't see how it could be done—the math didn't add up.

Ami was born in February, 1985. It was the most incredible feeling to hold my baby in my arms, to look down at that beautiful little face, and to have her fingers hold so tightly to my own. How could I bear to leave her and go back to work? I didn't want someone else to enjoy the pleasures of motherhood in my place. "How can this work out, Lord?" I asked constantly.

By April, the chief of police was inquiring as to when I would be returning to work, since I had taken a leave of absence. I prayed and told the Lord He would have to put it in Ken's heart to allow me to quit and stay at home with Ami. I then called Ken and told him we needed to talk that evening.

Presenting everything to him that night and both of us praying for God's direction, Ken finally stated, "Down deep in my heart, I don't really want you to go back to work either, so just give them your resignation. I don't know how we are going to make it, but somehow I guess we will." With Ken's approval, God gave me the best job could ever have asked for, and the desire of my heart.

I was a little nervous after handing in my resignation, but the Lord gave me a scripture I would stand on for the rest of my existence on earth. Philippians 4:19 says—"And my God shall supply all your need according to His riches in glory by Christ Jesus."

In the following weeks, I prayed that scripture over all the bills, over every situation, over everything. Every bill was met or paid in full—some were paid without our knowledge, in miraculous ways. Ken was given extra work details, people would bring us boxes of clothing for Ami, and food was given to us. God provided everything needed, even though our income was cut in half. We never discussed our situation with anyone else, but people brought over all kinds of things. Ken told me several months later, "We have more money now than we ever did when you were working." It really wasn't that we had more money. It was just God's provisions spent the right way and for the right motives.

I was able to stay at home and raise our children until the last one left our home, bound for ministry school. I praise Jesus for His many blessings and for giving me the desire of my heart. He is faithful in all things!

****

I went to the emergency room once, and sat there praying to God for the money to pay for the bill when it came due. Weeks later, a friend of mine and her mother wanted me to go to bingo with them. I wasn't much into bingo, but her mother kept asking me to go with them. Ken thought it would be a good chance for me to get out without the kids. So I went.

My friend and her mother both kept saying I was going to win that night. I was having a hard time just trying to keep up with the all numbers. But I won, and it was enough money to pay for the emergency room bill which arrived in the mail that very day, with enough left over to help another person in need at the time. I told my friend and her mother the story behind all of this, and they just couldn't get over how God made that happen! The scripture the Lord gave me that night was Proverbs 13:24, "But the wealth of the sinner is stored up for the righteous." It was important for me to realize He cares about every aspect of my life. What an awesome God we serve. He alone is worthy of all of our praise!

****

CHAPTER 7

I TRUST YOU, LORD

Suddenly, I was jolted back to the present and back to the reality of the Lord's question. "Cheryl, do you TRUST me?" Humbly I answered, "Yes, Lord Jesus, I really do trust You." He then told me my baby was with Him, so I knew the child I carried was dead. I was devastated. It broke my heart, and tears rolled down my face. He told me I must go through the physical part of it, but I was to keep my eyes on Him and not the situation. He said He would carry me through. He explained if I did this, He would carry me "above" the situation and He would cover me in His peace. I told Him I understood and trusted Him. That was the end of our conversation.

The next moment, terrible pains, like labor pains, shot through my body. I began hemorrhaging and had to stand in the bathtub. I yelled for our daughter, Jami, to call our neighbors, Chris and Bonnie, who responded immediately. Bonnie stayed with the children and made every attempt to contact Ken for hours. Chris drove me to the hospital and stayed with me the entire night until Ken could get there.

As we approached the hospital, I felt light-headed, almost ready to pass out. It was difficult to breath, and I had no strength since I lost a great deal of blood. The admitting attendant saw my condition and quickly called for people to assist. They were worried about my ashy gray color, and tried to find someone to get an IV going. The girl they found was either new or nervous, because she poked my arm about ten times, until they yelled at her, telling her to stop. They found another person, a man with a cross around his neck. I told the Lord, "I'll take him. Just make sure he does it right the first time." He had to use my right hand, which was painful, but he got it right the first time.

I heard the doctor tell Chris the situation was critical because of the loss of blood. Chris stayed with me, held my hand, and prayed.

What I remembered the most was the intense pain and telling Jesus, "I trust You. Please stay with me." I felt His peace come over me like a blanket. I don't recall how long everything took as I faded in and out, but my body was certainly relieved when everything was completed. All I wanted to do was fall asleep.

The doctor wanted me to see the baby, I suppose to allow reality to set in, but I didn't want to. I knew little Judah was with Jesus, and that was all that really mattered. Chris made sure they abided by my wishes.

I was so thankful God sent Chris with me because he went through a miscarriage with his wife before, and he had the knowledge and compassion to endure the same with me under the existing circumstances.

Ken finally arrived as they were moving me into a recovery area. He cried for our loss, but was also thankful I was doing better. He stayed with me until I fell asleep, and then went home to check on the children and to relieve Bonnie.

When I awoke, they sent a hospital representative from the pastoral care section in to talk with me. She began her speech with such remorseful words I had to stop her mid-sentence. I told her I knew my baby was with Jesus, which gave my soul such peace. I also told her He helped me through the critical parts concerning the situation throughout the night, and I was confident He would get me through all the emotional parts as well. I explained to her I knew my God whom I serve, and He has never let me down. We talked about this for several more minutes, and as she left the room, she turned around and said, "I came here to minister to you, but you have ministered to me!"

When Ken returned, he was able to talk to our doctor about letting me go home, as I didn't want to be there any longer. I just wanted to be home with my family. He agreed, on the condition I stay in bed for several days. There was no problem with that!

While in bed, the Lord spoke softly to me this scripture in Romans 8:28, "...all things work together for good to those who love God, to those who are the called according to His purpose." I didn't know how, but I knew God would turn this around for His glory. I knew my child was with the Lord. I would have worked and prayed all my life to make sure he belonged to Jesus, but He decided to take him home to be with Him at that point in time. I was at peace with that. I never resorted to being remorseful because He kept His promise to take me above the situation. I could only praise Him with my whole heart.

A friend of mine stopped by to see me with a book. Her inscription inside was Romans 8:28. Another friend gave me a card. Inside she had written the same scripture verse! I knew Jesus was confirming He would use this situation for good, to minister to others.

When I recovered, the Lord used the story of little Judah with many women who had gone through miscarriages. He asked them the same question, even after their ordeal, so they too would have the confidence in Him that all things work together for good to those who love Him. Many rededicated their hearts and lives to Him because they had been upset with Him for allowing their child to die. They were able to see God had a greater plan.

Praise did spring forth to the Lord from the short life of a little child He named Judah.

****

PART TWO

"Be still, and know that I am God" Psalm 46:10

CHAPTER 8

NEW PREPARATIONS

Ken and I celebrated our twenty-fifth wedding anniversary in October, 2006. He started a new position as the aircraft maintenance manager for a major university. We moved into our first house in over twelve years. Our daughters lived away from home, and we entered into a new season of our lives.

A new year began. One we hoped would be filled with new direction and new purpose, both in our lives and in our walk with Jesus. We anticipated the harvest field He presented us with, being in a college town, and working with students. We embraced the challenge of starting something brand new.

I began working on our new house to make it our home. We always dedicated our home to the Lord for a place of refuge for those who are in need. I remember thinking how big this house was for just two people, and I told the Lord He would just have to fill it up by bringing the people He needed to be there.

Ken was working hard, not only with the aircraft maintenance, but also as a consultant with another branch of the university in another city in starting up an aircraft maintenance program there. He was blessed with a hard working aircraft mechanic and student helpers who worked for him. I enjoyed stopping by to see Ken and watching how they all interacted. They were employees, yet like family. He respected each one, and they respected him.

Ken loved to fly, and had been a pilot for many years. One day, as we were enjoying a cup of coffee together, he said, "You know what I would like to do? I would like to one day fly around without a plane, just my body, like Superman! I think that would be cool!" He was completely serious. I looked at him with that wifely response of, "Right..." thinking maybe he'd been working a little too much. I left him to his thoughts.

Valentine's Day was special that year. He took me to a local restaurant and gave me beautiful flowers and a lovely card. He told me he loved me, he was glad that he married me, and he would do it all over again. He also said he would certainly be a different person had he not met me. Because of me, he said he belonged to Jesus, and his life was forever changed. He thanked me.

Ami's birthday was at the end of the month. Ken and I planned to visit her and Sara (both of them lived in North Carolina). Several days before leaving, he informed me he could not go due to an overload at work. I told him I didn't want to go without him and suggested we postpone the trip for a week or two. He insisted that I go without him because the girls "needed" me. I argued with him about it, but his mind was made up and his decision was final. He said if I didn't find an airline ticket on the internet he would find one for me. I thought his response to this was strange, as we always did things together or at least agreed upon what we were going to do. He just kept insisting I go and kept insisting the girls needed me to be there with them.

March 1, 2007, was a beautiful morning. The sun was shining as Ken drove me to the airport. We talked about the girls, what he had to work on that day, and made plans for me to call him throughout the day to see how he was doing. He dropped me off early since he had to be at work. I hugged and kissed him, and told him I really didn't want to go without him. He just said, "I know. It will be alright." We both said, "I love you." Then, he was gone.

I sat in the terminal, reading my Bible and praying. Sometimes, I looked up to watch people or pray for them as they passed by. In a still moment, I heard the Lord's voice asking me, "Cheryl, do you trust Me?" I wondered why He was asking me this question. *"I've been through this before."* Without any further hesitation I replied, "Yes, Lord Jesus, I really do trust you." He continued to say, "You will have to keep your eyes on Me, Cheryl, and I will bring you through this STORM. I will be with you and carry you through. You have to TRUST ME." I told Him I would trust Him. That was the end of our conversation—it was time to board the airplane.

"What storm was He talking about? My family has ups and downs, some easier than others, but we were not going through a storm at that moment. Storms to me implied fear, chaos, devastation, loss, uncertainty, and sometimes death. *"I know about storms. After all, I lived on a boat in Florida for the past ten years..."*

CHAPTER 9

WE CAN DO THIS

In 1995, Ken was able to retire from the police department early, so God directed us to sell our home and belongings and move onto a 50-foot sailboat in Florida. It was a drastic change of lifestyle for all of us, but it was the best move we ever made. We learned to live and to work together closely as a family, without the constant interruptions that we would normally have thought were so important or necessary. We had less clutter in our lives, and it was a wonderful feeling.

My only concern about living on the boat in Florida was the hurricanes and tropical storms. We had heard many "storm stories" from other boaters, but had not yet experienced our own. Our first experience with these storms came with Tropical Storm Josephine that presented itself in October, 1996. We prepared the boat and reinforced the lines to the pilings before the storm hit. (It was not a direct hit, but it was close enough for us to feel the effects of it.) The problem would not be the storm itself but the storm surge, which brought in a high level of water. Since our marina was not equipped with floating docks that rise with the water level, Ken decided we should stay on the boat so he could let the lines out as the water level rose, otherwise, there might be damage to the boat, the dock itself, or both. I wasn't enthusiastic about staying onboard during the storm, but Ken and I prayed and knew the Lord would protect us and take care of things. I remember Ken saying, "We can do this!"

The wind intensity picked up throughout the evening, gusting up to sixty miles per hour. Our boat lunged forward in the slip, straining the lines and pilings. The water level began to rise, as predicted and expected. Others stayed aboard their boats as well, but somehow that wasn't much comfort to me. The water moved rapidly through our little harbor off Tampa Bay and over the docks, so there was no getting off the boat, even if we wanted to. Time seemed to move forward slowly. It seemed like hours of having to listen to the howling of the wind, the water beating on the boat, and the lines straining as if they would snap at any moment. The boat shook and jolted back and forth with the enormous outburst of wind.

Ken was calm, keeping watch on everything and monitoring the radar. Ami and Sara, who were eleven and nine years old, were busy playing games in their cabin until they went to sleep. I was the only one who was nervous and jittery throughout the storm. Perhaps that was due to the fact that our children were aboard with us, and I didn't want anything to happen to harm them in any way. Maybe it was the fear of the danger involved. Somehow, I sensed the Lord was teaching me He is the calm in the midst of even the natural storms. I continued to pray throughout the night.

When the storm began to weaken, the surge was already well past the sea wall, and almost up to the marina office. The docks disappeared from sight because the height of the water concealed them. When Ken finally got off the boat to check the bow's position, he had to use a flashlight to make sure of the dock's boundaries. The water level was over his knees!

****

In November, 1996, as we were heading for our home port from a trip down south, we experienced a strong headwind and fought through waves that could bury the bow of the boat. We finally saw the Sunshine Skyway Bridge, the entrance into Tampa Bay, but with the wind working against us, it took a long while to get into the bay. Once under the bridge, we still faced several hours until we arrived back at port. (Under normal conditions, this same trip took only an hour). We also had to watch the navigational charts closely to make sure we had deep enough water for the boat and weren't drifting into shallow areas.

Suddenly, the engine whined for several minutes and then stopped. With as much caution as he could, Ken quickly made his way to the bow of the boat and threw the anchor overboard to stop us from drifting and going aground. He discovered that a bowline had loosened, traveled down the length of the keel, and wrapped itself around the propeller and shaft. I quickly called for Sea Tow, an organization that assists boaters in need, but they were twenty minutes away. Those minutes passed like hours as the boat tossed back and forth with the waves. It was the first and only time I felt a little sea sick, but I kept my composure in order to help Ken.

I prayed. I even spoke to the wind and the waves just like Jesus did to be still. They continued to rage on. I wanted so much to be out of this storm. I realized, though, that this was all about God's protection, even in the midst of the storm. He was with us and was taking care of us, even though we had to go through the turmoil.

When the Sea Tow operator arrived, he tied his boat next to ours, secured the lines, and proceeded to tow us back to our marina. The wind and waves were still contrary, so it was a rough ride back as well.

Once docked, we thanked the Lord for His mercy and protection. The scripture that came to me was in Psalm 107:23-31 which reads:

"Those who go down to the sea in ships, who do business on great waters, they see the works of the Lord, and His wonders in the deep. For He commands and raises the stormy wind, which lifts up the waves of the sea. They mount up to the heavens, they go down again to the depths; their soul melts because of trouble. They reel to and fro, and stagger like a drunken man, and are at their wits' end. Then they cry out to the Lord in their trouble, and he brings them out of the distresses. He calms the storm, so that the waves are still. Then they are glad because they are quiet; so He guides them to their desired haven. Oh, that men would give thanks to the Lord for His goodness, and for His wonderful works to the children of men!"

Another praise report was no damage to the engine, propeller, or shaft. After a complete check over, it started right up!

****

We took a trip to Ft. Myers beach in July, 1998, and found a nice anchorage in Matanzas Pass. It was a wide basin, and was the main harbor for the area. We set the main anchor, but due to the swift current, the boat began to drag. We pulled up the main anchor then reset it. Ken also put the secondary anchor out just to make sure the boat wouldn't drift. I prayed that God would be the anchor to our boat and not allow it to move out of its position.

After spending the day at the beach, we returned to the boat. Ken turned on the radar, as we noticed storm clouds were moving in (which is typical in Florida in the summer). Within a few minutes, the wind picked up, and the storm blew in. The rain was heavy, along with lightning and thunder. The current in the basin picked up significantly, and the boat strained on the anchor lines. Heavy rains kept us from seeing outside clearly, so I just kept asking the Lord to keep our boat safe during the storm and to keep the anchors set. After a few hours, the storm subsided. When we went outside to check on the boat's position, we were still in the same spot. Several of the other boats lost their anchor's grip and landed near the seawall.

The next day, pulling up the anchors proved difficult. They were anchored so well to the basin's floor that it took us over an hour to break them free. The experience showed a great analogy of how Jesus, our Anchor, keeps us in place during life's storms, so we are secure in Him.

****

We crossed Lake Okeechobee several times with normally great weather. In the summer of 2001, this particular crossing was not one of those times. We had just made it under the railroad bridge at Port Mayaca, heading out to the open lake for the crossing to Clewiston. I was at the helm while Ken was relaxing near the bow of the boat. It was a beautiful day and the water was calm and peaceful. About the time we hit the midpoint of open water, I remember thinking, "This is the calmest I have ever seen this lake." It was like glass. Literally, it was the calm before the storm, as I noticed small waves mounting and heading toward the boat. The dark clouds and extreme wind followed quickly. It was extremely difficult to spot the channel markers, even with binoculars. Ferocious waves slammed the hull. As I watched a small powerboat race past us to the channel, for the first time I wished for a powerboat instead of a sailboat.

We prayed and asked God to again keep us in the palm of His hand and to guide us safely to Clewiston. We asked Him to keep the boat from any damage or from running aground in the shallow lake, and that He get us through this storm to a safe haven. Then we thanked Him for doing so and pressed on through the storm.

Once in the channel, trying to maneuver our large sailboat was complicated. The wind pressed against the starboard side, causing us to strain at the helm in order to keep the boat in the narrow channel. Ken was at the helm, and I struggled to find each channel marker with the binoculars so that we could stay on course and not go aground, as the wind pushed us toward the shore. I remember thanking and praising God there was no rain involved with this storm, or we would have been hard pressed to find the markers!

As we made our final turn to Clewiston, the wind began to diminish and the clouds lightened. I was so relieved to see the 20 foot dike that surrounds the lake and that opens up to the boat docks there. We arrived by the hand of God, to a safe haven.

That is not the end of this story, however. The next morning, while traveling down the river portion of the Okeechobee Waterway, near La Belle, a mini storm occurred that lasted no more than fifteen minutes. During this storm, however, the steering cable broke. Ken quickly threw the anchor out to stop the boat from drifting into the shoreline. Instead of complaining, we both prayed and thanked God that it didn't happen the day before when we were in the perilous storm on Lake Okeechobee. That would have been disastrous. God had compassion on us in this situation also because we found a bicycle cable in one of the lockers we used to repair the cable until we got to Ft. Myers. How great our God is!

****

One summer afternoon in 2002, as I was standing on top of a houseboat at our marina, I noticed a funnel cloud quickly form and descend just a few miles away. It was interesting because it only seemed to last for a few minutes, and then it disappeared. Later that day, when we drove into town, we witnessed the destruction it caused. Houses damaged, trees uprooted, signs twisted and bent over, traffic lights dismantled, fences torn down, and numerous other thing destroyed. It reminded me how fragile life is and how things can change in a matter of seconds.

It was also a good reminder that Jesus is our stability through every one of life's storms, and that He is our safe refuge.

****

The year 2004 was the year of the hurricanes in Florida. It began with Hurricane Charley. Everyone made the necessary preparations with the approach of this hurricane. The marina management made sure double lines secured every boat (this marina had floating docks). People left for shelter on the other side of the state. Store shelves emptied due to people stocking up before the storm. Long lines formed at every gas station as cars filled up in preparation. Homes and businesses boarded up.

Ken worked as a flight school manager and airplane mechanic at the local airport.

He prepared the airplanes, and tried to fit as many as he possibly could into a large hangar. (I believe there were twelve airplanes stuffed into the space of that hangar.) Larger planes flew out of the state for safety. One lone airplane stayed tied on the field, uncared for.

I remember going around our marina, praying God's protection over every boat, touching each one. I prayed for every person, and for the entire property. I prayed over Ken's boss' house, where we stayed during the storm and the hangar at the airport. I prayed Psalm 91 over all of us, and over the entire area.

That morning, August 13, 2004, Ken made sure the boat was as secure as possible, and we left for the home provided for us. We had taken valuables off the boat already, so we brought only clothes, personal items, a flashlight, and an emergency radio we used on the boat.

The morning weather started off cloudy and breezy, but then the winds began to gust. This would be no ordinary day.

Hurricane Charley was predicted to make landfall near Tampa. However, Charley strengthened quickly and jumped from a Category 2 to a Category 4 hurricane in just a few hours. It also made a sharp turn towards the northeast, heading for the Fort Myers area.

Fierce winds raged and heavy rains fell. It made a sound like a freight train barreling through the area. It was the strangest sound I had ever heard. We listened to the radio throughout the storm, trying to keep informed. There were palm branches and debris flying in all directions. At one point, as we stood at the back of the house near a balcony, Ken observed the neighbor's large patio enclosure, which was shaking and swaying from the force of the wind, and said, "That's not going to last very long." Within seconds, the enclosure exploded into the air, its many pieces flying in every direction. We watched as the winds snapped palm trees in half, and uprooted large live oak trees.

Bits and pieces of unidentified homes flew through the air, abandoned cars pushed down the street, street signs bent over, and light posts pulled right out of the ground.

By the mercy of God, Hurricane Charley was a fast-moving hurricane, so by evening, it passed through our area. When we walked out of the house, there was water up to our knees in the street. Devastation was everywhere. There was damage to every home in the neighborhood with one exception.

The house we stayed in and prayed over suffered no damage.

We attempted to drive back to our marina. There were no traffic lights operating. In fact, no lights anywhere were operating. The only lights were those of the cars of people trying to make it back to their homes. Telephone poles and trees littered the roads. Some roads were not even passable. Shingles and sections of roofs were torn off houses. Windows not boarded up were broken and destroyed. Signs and billboards were demolished. It literally looked like a war zone!

What would have normally taken about twenty minutes instead took us several hours, but we finally returned to our marina. We found the marina and boat unscathed. In fact, the only damage to any of our marina boats was a fly bridge that came loose from an older boat and sank. Our boat withstood the hurricane force winds without any problems, due to the hand of our God upon it. We were also one of the fortunate ones because we had filed our water tank up on the boat to make it heavier in the slip, and we had a generator aboard so we could run the air conditioning and electric. After the sheer exhaustion of the day, we thanked God for His protection and provisions and fell asleep.

The next day, Ft. Myers looked as if it had been bombed overnight. Punta Gorda, about twenty minutes away, suffered the greatest damage from the storm, so news media focused most of their reporting there.

A gentleman asked Ken to check the damage to his airplane in a hangar at the Punta Gorda airport. Ken and I both went. We were not prepared for the scene we witnessed that morning. A set of airplane hangars blown away, one plane hanging upside down in its hangar with its tail stuck in the roof, other planes twisted around like pretzels and damaged beyond repair, and one had a piece of wood pierced through its wing. Damage and debris were everywhere. Most of the airplanes were destroyed—like that lone plane we last saw standing in the field, or they were damaged severely. It appeared a war had been fought, and lost, there. Perhaps that was the truth of it. I had never witnessed such a sight. Ironically, I recorded these images at the airport on a disposable camera I fished out of the water at the marina that morning!

In town and around the area, the aftermath of the hurricane proved to be the most chaotic. There was nothing to buy in the stores, as the shelves were bare, and there was no electric to be able to run the refrigeration. Little gasoline remained throughout the southern part of the state due to people filling up before the hurricane. The state activated the National Guard, and they provided assistance in various ways, especially in traffic control, since there were no operating traffic lights. People had no electric for their homes or businesses. The power companies sent convoys of white trucks throughout the area in order to get the power back up again, but this took weeks. Police, fire, and emergency personnel worked nonstop to regain some type of order. Sadly, many insurance companies delayed their responses to claims so people went many months without having much needed assistance.

The Christian community rallied together helping those in need and witnessing for Jesus. Many other people and organizations were also involved. All worked together for the common cause. They made sure people were fed and given shelter. They gave to others when they themselves had also suffered loss. They worked together to clean up and rebuild. They knew they had to move forward, whether by a little step or a big one, and so they did, by God's grace. God's help and blessings came to them as they helped and blessed others in need.

Just when it seemed like we were making a little progress in the clean-up of Hurricane Charley, another hurricane, named Frances, developed in the Atlantic Ocean. Although initially forecasted to head northeast toward Bermuda, its track shifted westward toward Florida's east coast. The large, Category 2 hurricane hit Florida in the early hours of September 5, 2004.

Again, we made preparations on the west coast of Florida for this hurricane. We continued to pray and ask for God's protection, over us and over all the people of Florida. This time, we stayed in a local motel and waited out the storm.

The wind and rain came, but we did not have the devastation as we did with Hurricane Charley. The problem was the damage that had already occurred to homes and property continued with the new storm. Mold set in, with flooding and water damage at an all time high in our area. What may have been salvageable was now damaged beyond repair.

The east coast definitely received the worst of Hurricane Frances. The marina where we lived in Fort Pierce was destroyed. Homes, apartment complexes, and condos were ravaged by the storm. Trees uprooted and foliage completely wiped out. Piers were torn apart to mere posts. Beaches were eroded.

Around September 11, Hurricane Ivan became a major threat again to the west coast of Florida as it passed through western Cuba as a Category 5 hurricane. Although we did not receive the full impact of that hurricane (it made landfall in Alabama and Northern Florida), we again had to prepare for the worst, as it again brought the intense wind and rain with it.

After making a complete loop over the Atlantic Ocean, Hurricane Jeanne began heading westward toward the east coast of Florida as a Category 3 hurricane. On September 25, Jeanne made landfall just two miles from where Hurricane Frances struck a few weeks earlier. This hurricane brought near record flood levels throughout its path. Again, the pounding of this destructive force sent people staggering in its aftermath.

By this time, all of Florida, as well as other states touched by these hurricanes, were reeling from the damage, deaths, flooding, and expense they had caused. Throughout these devastating storms, the hand of God kept us safe and protected on our boat. We realized it was not because we were any more loved or cared for than anyone else, but we had to trust Him with every fiber of our being because we were very vulnerable in our situation living on a boat. We trusted the Lord and relied upon Him. We also realized it was our responsibility to help others less fortunate through the difficult times.

We took an airplane ride after the hurricane season, and were amazed at the damage we viewed from the air. So many homes had blue tarps over the roofs, one small airport on Pine Island had been demolished, a new inlet had been cut from the Gulf of Mexico by Hurricane Charley's path, mobile home parks wiped out, areas flooded, vegetation stripped away, and the list went on. It made me look at storms in a whole new way.

Living through the 2004 hurricane season made me realize how fragile life is, but our God is more powerful than any force on earth, even the strongest hurricane. I know He kept us in the palm of His hand, He made sure that we were provided for, and nothing of ours was lost or destroyed. Most of all, I glorify Him as God, the Ruler of heaven and earth and everything contained therein. I will always thank Him and trust Him no matter what.

****

CHAPTER 10

FLYING THROUGH THE STORMS

When the Lord spoke to me as I waited for that flight to Charlotte, I pondered His words even as I boarded the plane. Maybe this would be a rough ride, passing through a storm, but somehow it seemed like something much more complicated than riding on a plane.

It has always been my routine before I board any flight, whether on a jet or in our own personal airplane, to pray and ask the Lord to put that particular airplane in the palm of His hand, and to keep everyone on board safe from danger and disaster. I also pray that if there is any danger whatsoever, He would not allow the plane to take off. Many times I have been thankful I prayed when He took care of extreme situations.

Aboard the plane bound for Atlanta, I sat next to a young man in his early thirties. We talked for a few minutes, and then he fell asleep. The plane took off on time, and it appeared to be a normal flight for the first twenty minutes. Then we experienced turbulence that was relentless. It was the worst I had ever experienced, and I flew quite a bit. We jerked from side to side, jolted upward, and dropped downward. This continued throughout the entire course of the flight. It seemed every bolt holding the plane together would come loose. Several people were frightened and held tightly to their armrests. One little child started to cry. I believe the "fasten your seatbelt" sign was on the entire flight, and the pilot apologized for the inconvenience of the turbulence on several occasions. The gentleman next to me woke up and stated, "Man, this is like the plane ride from hell!" I think most people would have agreed!

When we landed in Atlanta, we learned all the flights were delayed going in most directions due to severe storms (tornados) occurring in Missouri, Alabama, and Georgia. The airport was overcrowded with passengers stranded until later flights could be boarded. It was impossible to get something to eat because the vendors were overwhelmed with the volume of people they had to deal with at one time.

I called Ken to let him know I was safe in Atlanta but my flight was delayed to Charlotte. We talked about the turbulence and the tornados for a few minutes and then went on with other conversation. Before we hung up, he prayed for me. He said he would call me later when I arrived in Charlotte.

I sat and watched people get angry and complain about the situation. I wondered how many even knew

God kept them safe from the turmoil in the skies. "Are we all so caught up in ourselves that we can't see even the smallest things that God does for us? Do we even care?" These thoughts came randomly as I sat waiting and watching.

Finally, I boarded the flight to Charlotte. The turbulence was again a factor. I thanked God it was a shorter flight. Knowing Sara would be at the airport to meet me, made the turbulence seem less significant. I couldn't wait to get my feet back on solid ground again.

CHAPTER 11

THE CALL

Sara picked me up from the airport. I dropped her off at work and went to check on brakes for her car. We were supposed to drive to Wilmington in the morning, but I didn't trust her brakes. After going to several places for estimates, I called Ken to find out what he wanted me to do concerning the car. We talked for several minutes, but then someone came into his office, so he had to go. When I got off the phone, I wished he were there with me so he could take care of the car situation.

I had a slight headache and realized I had not eaten anything since breakfast, so I drove to a local restaurant. Ken called back as I drove into the parking lot. He said he wanted to call me back before he went to play racquetball with our pastor. He proceeded to tell me how his day went. He told me to make sure I got something to eat. He came up with a plan to get the car fixed in Wilmington. Before he hung up, he said, "Now I don't want you to worry. Everything will be just fine. I love you. Tell the girls I love them. I will talk to you later."

I felt a little uneasy at the restaurant, like something wasn't quite right, but I shrugged it off as being overly hungry and restless from the events of the day. I was also extremely tired because I hadn't slept very well the night before.

Shortly thereafter, I picked up Sara from work, and we drove to her apartment. Her roommates had several classmates and friends over for dinner, so we walked in and tried not to disturb them. I went into Sara's bedroom, set my travel bag down on the floor, and at that moment, my cell phone rang. The man on the line did not immediately identify himself but asked me a series of questions.

"Do you know Ken Cunnagin?

"Yes," I replied.

"Are you in town?"

"No, who is this?" I asked.

"Is Ken the aircraft maintenance manager at the university?"

"Yes, who is this?" I asked again, thinking that it was someone looking for Ken (I was on the verge of hanging up on him).

His last question was, "Are you Cheryl, his wife?"

"Yes," I replied.

He then proceeded into an area of conversation that I could never have been prepared to hear or receive at that moment. "This is the county coroner, and I must inform you that Ken has passed away."

With all of my police experience, as soon as he said "coroner", I knew Ken had died before he could say the rest.

Suddenly, I could not breathe, my heart started racing, and fell to my knees on the floor, not able or wanting to process what I had just been told. I asked him if he could call me back in a minute or two, at which time he said he would. I gasped for breath. I felt like I was having a heart attack.

Sara saw me on the floor and heard me crying, "No, God! No!" She knelt down by me and asked, "Mom! What's the matter? What's wrong?" I could barely utter a word, but somehow I managed to tell her. The look on her face was more than I could bear as her mother at that moment. She began to scream and cry until she was hysterical, and the friends who were present in the apartment came to her assistance. I asked them to help her because I wasn't able. The phone rang again. It was the coroner. I asked him what happened and he related the following events:

Ken was driving to the recreation center at the university. As he turned in front of the center, he must have felt something coming on with his heart because he pressed his foot on the brake pedal to stop the car and immediately slumped over the steering wheel. The car stopped in the street. A person passing by saw the incident and called the police immediately.

When the police and paramedics arrived, they lifted him out of the car, put him in the ambulance, and tried to resuscitate him as they traveled to the hospital. He was pronounced dead at the hospital of a heart attack.

He wanted to ask me a few questions, but again I had to ask him if he could call back, as Sara needed to talk to me, and he could hear she was not doing well with the news. He said he would.

I called Ami. She didn't answer her phone, so I left a message for her to call me right away. A minute later, she called back, noting the distress in my voice and wondering what had happened. I told her. Ami began to cry and yelled, "No! No! How did this happen?" She was quite upset, so I asked to speak to her roommate. "Could you drive Ami here tonight so we can get back to Ohio by the morning? I don't want her to drive by herself." She assured me she would and they would start for Charlotte immediately.

I then called Jami, Ken's daughter, but she did not answer her telephone. I left a message for her, informing her of her dad's death, hoping that someone would be with her when she got it.

Informing my children of an event like this is something I never want to do again. Seeing the anguish on their faces and hearing the sorrow from their heart is something that is not easily forgotten. It pierced my heart.

From that point on, the cell phone was on a continuous ring. I called my sister, Carole, so she could call the rest of my family, and I called Ken's father so he could contact his side of the family. I called our pastor to ask if he could help get the car back home (he was the police chaplain) and to let out dog outside. The coroner called back again, then Ken's boss, family members… It was all a blur. Thoughts were not even registering at that point.

Someone called an advisor from the school of ministry where Sara and the other roommates attended. She was a tremendous help to both Sara and I. She stayed throughout the evening, and left only after Ami arrived and we started back to Ohio. As we talked, I remember telling her I would praise the Lord, even through this storm. I told her even though I did not understand everything, I knew Ken was with Jesus, and I would continue to trust the Lord.

The young people stayed with us until Ami and her roommate arrived around three o'clock in the morning. A good friend of Sara's offered to drive us back since she didn't think it was wise for any of us to drive at that point. The four of us drove throughout the night. It was the longest and loneliest trip of my life.

Thoughts of our life together flooded my mind. "I had just been with him a few hours back. I just talked with him. *Now he's not here anymore. I will have to live my life without him—how can that be done?"* I remembered all the things we had done recently. His sweet smile kept coming into my thoughts. I was already lonely without him. I knew a part of me died that day too.

CHAPTER 12

YOU SAID YOU WOULD TRUST ME

The sun rose the next morning as we drove back home and its light cast on every location that held a memory of Ken in our town and the surrounding area. We passed the airport where he had dropped me off the morning before and kissed me goodbye for the last time. The restaurant where he took me a week before, the place where we often went for coffee, the motel we stayed in when he interviewed for the university job…everything was a vivid memory of our life together, a life that was now no longer.

As we approached our home, I noticed the garage door open, and our car that Ken drove parked inside. My brothers, Steve and Chris, were waiting for us to arrive. Sara, Ami, and I were weeping. It was difficult to walk in the house and see his glasses, keys, and coat sitting on the counter. He had also picked up two movies from the video store. The house seemed so empty, so lonely. His favorite chair was empty. The book he was reading sat on the table beside it. On the chair in our bedroom, after changing into gym clothes, were the clothes he wore to work that day.

Our pastor, Dave, came over to take us to the morgue to identify Ken's body. I must say even my experience as a police officer did not prepare me for having to walk through that door. He was the love of my life, and my best friend. He was everything to me, so to see his body in the morgue caused more pain than I ever imagined possible. The gentleman handed me his personal belongings, including his wallet. Pain gripped my heart so tightly; I couldn't breathe. Streams of tears rolled down my face.

Sara did not come with us because I felt like she couldn't handle the situation, but Ami insisted on coming. The difficulty of her seeing her dad was heartbreaking and painful. She cried for a long time. Just a day earlier, he had wished her a happy birthday and prayed with her for God's plan and blessings to come forth in her life.

We returned home to a house full of family. Everything moved so fast my mind was in a fog. I couldn't remember questions people asked or where things were. My glasses and phone were lost numerous times. I had not slept since the night before. I don't remember eating or being hungry enough to eat.

I went to the funeral home with Dave, Sara, Ami, and three of my brothers. The funeral director was very kind, but a great deal of information was required, and to make those types of decisions under that level of grief and stress was difficult to say the least. I even forgot to include Ken's grandmother and step brother's names in the obituary notice.

More people came over to the house, and food arrived from the neighborhood and the university. A number of the girls' friends from North Carolina came up as well, so there were people everywhere in the house that night. I prayed, "Lord Jesus, I am so tired. If you would please help me find somewhere to lie down, I would appreciate it." Ami and Sara were already sleeping in my bed, as they had given their rooms up to others, so I pushed them over to one side and found enough space for my body to fit. I fell fast asleep from exhaustion.

The next couple of days blurred together. I could not focus. Only Jesus knew the overwhelming depth of sorrow that I felt in my heart. Never had I cried so much as I cried during those first few days. Even though I was surrounded by many family members and friends, I was alone.

It was then the Lord began to speak to my heart saying, "Cheryl, you said you would trust Me. I promised you I would bring you through this storm, but you have to keep your eyes on Me and trust Me.

I responded by saying out loud, "I trust you Lord Jesus, and I am hanging on to you with every fiber of my being."

God sent Mo from the university over to the house. I met her several weeks before when Ken introduced us at a party hosted by the dean. We sat down in the living room, and she gave me the opportunity just to talk. I don't even remember what I talked about, but at that moment, I needed to talk more than anything else. I asked if she could stay a while longer because it was a release just to talk, and she graciously agreed. God sent the right person at the right time, to listen and to help me.

I remember standing on the stair leading upstairs, looking in to the living room at all the people there, thinking, "Well, Lord, you filled up this house, just like I asked You to, only I didn't realize it would start in Ken's behalf." Jesus then assured me from that point forward He would continue to fill it.

The outpouring of love God sent to me and my family was overwhelming. We received many cards, some from people we didn't know but who knew Ken. Flowers came from everywhere. Phone calls were abundant. Food came from many people. Money also came from my family and other sources. The hugs, yes, the hugs—they were the most wonderful gifts of compassion people had to offer. I appreciated every gesture of love shown to my daughters and me.

Many people prayed for us. For the first time in my life, I could actually feel the power of the prayers of God's people lifting us up. It wasn't just a sense of that, but an actual feeling. I imagined it to be like a force field connected to the power of God lifting us up and carrying us through. I was totally in awe and acutely aware of the prayers every single day.

I talked to Jesus continually. In the lonely hours of one night, with tears streaming down my face, and deep sorrow hidden in my heart, I prayed a prayer from the depth of my soul to ask Him this:

"Lord, if someone so precious to me had to be taken out of my life (and I'm ok with that because I know he is with You), then I want something precious back from You. I want souls for the Kingdom of Heaven—not just a few, Jesus. I want a lot, a great multitude. So, here I am. Send me. I'm now free to go wherever You need me to go. I will go to whomever you send me to. Please make sure this harvest of souls comes in."

Two viewings were held at the funeral home, due to the large number of people traveling from out of town and people working at the university. Both of them were completely filled with people. I don't recall just how many people I talked with and hugged, but I certainly appreciated each one. I knew they came because they respected and loved Ken in his life, and now showed us that same love in the wake of his death. It seemed that everyone had such wonderful memories to share of the gentle and kindhearted Ken. One student called him the "gentle giant," which I thought was quite fitting. Others left notes of their feelings for Ken and spoke of how he had made an impact in their lives.

Our daughter, Ami, along with Pastor Dave, presided over the funeral. I asked Pastor Dave to include a call for those touched by the Holy Spirit to receive Jesus Christ as their personal Savior. At least thirty people responded to that call! The seed of salvation planted in their hearts and lives had come to life. It reminded me of what Jesus said in John 12:24:

> "Most assuredly, I say to you, unless a grain of wheat falls into the ground and dies, it remains alone; but if it dies, it produces much grain (fruit)."

Even though there was great sorrow in my heart at the thought of going on with life without Ken, to watch the Lord's resurrection of lives from the dead (spiritually) was by far the most urgent of needs. That day, I was forever grateful to Him for adding names in His Book of Life.

CHAPTER 13

LIVING LIFE IN THE STORM

The funeral would have been the eye of the storm, where there is relative calm. It made me reflect on what God was perfecting through the midst of this tragic moment in time. However, the intensity of this "storm" has continued for months. In fact, "micro-storms" have developed within this major event. Situations I would never have wanted to think about, let alone go through, tried to press down on me: depression, loneliness, deep sorrow, anxiety, financial situations, legal situations, fatigue, sleepless nights, loss of appetite, wondering where to begin my new life and when, and a host of other things. Compounded with that, my daughters, Ami and Sara, moved back home with their own set of "storms" they were dealing with. Some days I didn't know if it was worth getting out of bed. At the end of the day, I looked forward to going to bed, closing my eyes, and hoping it would all be over with when I woke up again. This truly has been the most difficult situation I have ever had to live through or deal with in my life.

Once someone asked me how I was doing and what I was experiencing with all of this, and I described it to them in this way:

"It's like I am dog paddling in the ocean, with no land in sight, and no direction to actually go. From nowhere, an enormous wave emerges, breaking down over the top of me, and pushes me down deep into the water. I fight hard to swim back to the surface before I run out of air, and when I make it, I gasp for every breath. I dog paddle again to stay afloat. Then, another wave emerges, and the process repeats again and again. That is what it feels like. Only Jesus is keeping me afloat."

I want to be completely honest and real about what I had to endure, not to complain, but to help others see and understand that even as Christians we face hardships, pain, sufferings, and devastating things. It is not God's purpose to destroy us, but through His love and wisdom, change us into His image. In fact, these types of situations are opportunities for God to show His mighty power and love on our behalf. Second Corinthians 4:6-11 puts it this way:

"For it is the God who commanded light to shine out of darkness, who has shone in our hearts to give the light of the knowledge of the glory of God in the face of Jesus Christ. But we have this treasure in earthen vessels that the excellence of the power may be of God and not us. We are hard-pressed on every side, yet not crushed; we are perplexed, but not in despair; persecuted, but not forsaken; struck down, but not destroyed—always carrying about in the body the dying of the Lord Jesus, that the life of Jesus also may be manifested in our body. For we who live are always delivered to death for Jesus' sake, that the life of Jesus also may be manifested in our mortal flesh."

Through all of this, He constantly reminded me, "Cheryl, you said you would trust Me. I will bring you through this storm as I have promised. Though you don't understand now, you will have the understanding afterward. Just keep your eyes on me and trust Me." His gentle, loving words call to my spirit and calm me. My response to Him is always, "Yes, Lord Jesus, I still trust You. Thank You for not letting go of me."

I know I have nowhere else to go but to Him. I know nothing can separate me from His love for me. He has never left me or forsaken me. The scripture in Psalm 23—"though I walk through the valley of the shadow of death, I will fear no evil, for You are with me"—has become a part of my walk with Him. I confess He alone is my refuge, my fortress, my God, and in Him will I trust.

PART THREE

"To everything there is a season, a time for every purpose under heaven..."

Ecclesiastes 3:1

CHAPTER 14

JAMAICA

Several years ago, my sister, Karen, and I were praying at our home church in Florida at her ordination. The Lord spoke to me and told me He would send me all over the world to preach the gospel, but first He would send me to Jamaica. He also told me Ken would not be going with me, which at the time I thought was strange. I remember thinking I didn't know anything about Jamaica, but there was an excitement in my spirit. At the ordination, our pastor asked Karen and I to come up and give a testimony. I shared what the Lord spoke to me concerning sending me around the world to preach, starting at Jamaica. When I spoke it forth, it was set in motion and sealed in my heart.

Over the years, I have sought out information on Jamaica, found maps and studied them, looked up mission trips, researched flights, dreamed and prayed for Jamaica, and looked for the opening in God's perfect timing. Nothing was right, until February 10, 2008.

God promised me "new beginnings" in 2008. After 2007, I looked desperately for them. Having lived through the darkest and lowest place of my life, I was ready for something new. Jamaica kept coming to my mind, and it was stirring deeply in my heart.

My friend, Mo, took me out for coffee one afternoon. She told me I needed to get away, to go somewhere new. She asked me where I would go. Without hesitation, I said, "Jamaica." She encouraged me to check out the last minute travel deals to see what I could find. I did and found a great deal at a resort. I called another precious friend, Judy, to pray with me about the situation that only the perfect will of God would be done in this before I decided. He wanted me to continue trusting Him—even in Jamaica. That was Wednesday night—I left on Sunday morning!

Not everyone was as excited as I was about the trip. Some people thought I was acting out of the ordinary, a little crazy maybe. Others were concerned I was going by myself. Still others were concerned about the poverty and crime. If I learned anything throughout my walk with the Lord it is when He sends you forth, it's in your heart to go, and it doesn't matter what is being said by others who don't understand. When He gives you the go ahead, it's time to move!

Flying into the airport at Montego Bay, Jamaica, I remember thinking to myself, "This is the coolest thing I have ever done. I also prayed, "Thank you Jesus, for sending me here. Let Your will be done here and in my life. Use me however You see fit."

Trusting the Lord in this journey started immediately. Upon picking up a car at the airport, I asked them if they had any maps.

"No," was the reply.

"Could you tell me how to get to the resort?" I asked.

"Just go out here and turn left for about a half an hour," was the response.

"What is the name of the street I need to look for?"

"No name. There might be a sign." Frustrated, I asked if there was a landmark nearby.

"Just follow the road toward Falmouth."

I then prayed and asked the Holy Spirit to guide me directly there, since I had no idea where I was going.

I learned how to drive on the right side of the car and on the left side of the road rather quickly. I also learned a few Jamaican words I probably did not want to repeat as I was driving. Driving lessons and language lessons rolled into one in Jamaica. I discovered the horn is the main component on every car, and drivers like to get within inches (literally) of your car when they pass you. No wonder all the cars looked like they belonged in a demolition derby!

Thanks to the guidance of the Holy Spirit, I was able to find the resort. They gave me a beautiful room directly on the beach. I loved hearing the waves crashing to the shore, especially in the evening. Also, there were so many different shade of blue (my favorite color), from the vibrant colors of the ocean water to the vivid blue of the sky. I felt such wonderful peace for the first time in a long while.

I began meeting employees at the resort, who were so gracious and friendly. I loved getting acquainted with them. They always had smiles on their faces and kind words to speak.

That evening, I pulled out my music. I found a song about taking shackles off and started dancing around the room for several hours just praising God. I literally felt shackles falling off me. I knew I could do the work God had sent me there to do. It was overwhelming, but exciting at the same time.

Each day, I prayed for God to use me and send me exactly where He needed me to go. I also prayed for Him to prepare people's hearts to receive Jesus as their Savior and Lord. I asked Him to confirm His word through signs, wonders and miracles so the Jamaican people would know His awesome power. I also prayed for His protection.

Ocho Rios was my first destination. Cruise ships come into port there, so there is always a great deal of activity and people present. The day I was there, five cruise ships came in. Many Jamaicans sell their trinkets and wares along the street. I listened to them first, and then asked if they knew Jesus. Most of them did not, so I was able to talk with them and introduce them to their Savior through prayer. It was awesome to have so many people who wanted to hear what you had to tell them about Jesus, and then want to accept Him.

A couple of shop owners asked me about my "footprints" necklace that I wore. They had never heard the story, so I told them about it and about Jesus. They wanted to look it up on the computer to learn more.

Upon returning to the resort, several employees helped carry my things back to the room. One of them wanted prayer because he wasn't doing so well that day. Others came along and we talked about Jesus. They were all so hungry to know Him. It was like a plant in dry soil. I was amazed at what God was doing.

That night, I thanked God for all He did in the lives of the people I met and prayed with. I asked Him to continue to pour out His Spirit upon the Jamaican people so truly a great harvest would come from the tiny country.

He also gave me a song that day, so I danced, sang and prayed to the Lord for several hours. The presence of the Lord was so powerful even the housekeeping ladies made mention of "something special that was in my room" when they came in the next morning.

After breakfast, the Holy Spirit sent me to Negril. It was about a two-hour drive there, so I prayed, listened to my music, and enjoyed the countryside. It amazed me to see the contrast between the beauty of the ocean on one side of the street, and the shacks and poverty on the other side. I wondered how poverty had taken such a grip on the island and on the spirits of the people who lived there.

I decided to a stroll through town, browsing through all the different shops. One shop appeared particularly interesting to me because the outside was so colorful, so I went in. The young girl showed me T-shirts, coffee mugs, jewelry, and everything else she hoped I would purchase. Then she became silent, studying me for a few minutes.

Finally, she stated that I looked like I knew Jesus and asked if I was a Christian. I told her I was, and her face lit up. She said she loved Jesus too, but a demonic spirit tormented her mind. She said she prayed, but it kept coming back. We talked about her situation. I told her Jesus was the Deliverer, and explained He wanted her to be free. We began to pray, and Jesus set her free right then. She was so excited and said God told her she would be a missionary for Him. She wrote down her address and made me promise to write. She also asked if I could send her a Bible because hers had missing pages. I promised her I would.

The beach was down the street. I found a parking spot and had to walk up a path to reach the beach. Several ladies sitting near the entrance asked me if I wanted braids in my hair. Since my hair is short, I thought maybe it was joke, but I decided to let them put five braids in so I could take a picture and show it to my daughters and friends. In the meantime, I asked them if they knew Jesus. Two of them said they did, but then began "telling" on the other three, stating they were sinners who needed "talking to." I told them about Jesus the Savior and that He had a plan for their lives. They prayed with me to receive Him into their hearts and then left in a hurry.

In the next couple of minutes, they returned with a group of Jamaican people they had rounded up on the beach. They said, "Cheryl, here are more sinners to pray for!" So I talked and prayed with them. Meanwhile, the ladies I first prayed with put aloe on my arms and legs so I wouldn't get sunburned!

The last man they brought to me was a big guy called "Big John". He glared at me while the ladies advised me "he's the biggest sinner of them all." I prayed under my breath for the words to speak to this man because he didn't seem very receptive. I looked in his eyes for a few minutes and then I said, "John— that's my dad's name. I think it's a great name. I like it." Immediately, he broke out in a grin from ear to ear. Then he said, "Now I will hear what you have to say. *"Thank you, Jesus."* He listened and prayed to receive Jesus as the Lord of his life.

The ladies then pulled a woman off the beach to put braids in her hair and asked her if she knew Jesus. She said "no," and they looked at me and said, "Cheryl, here's another sinner." I talked with her about the love of Jesus and prayed with her as well.

My time in Negril was up since I had a two-hour drive back. Big John walked me to my car and made me promise to come back and see all of them when I returned to Jamaica. I promised him I would.

Back at the resort, several of the employees, who were now friends, came up to my room and we talked about Jesus. Later in the evening, as I walked around the compound, many of them found me, wanting prayer or just to talk for a few minutes. I loved their kind hearts and warm smiles. I often thought it was just as important for me to be in Jamaica because of the kindness they showed to me every day. God used them to help me too.

The next day, I ran into one of the shop owners from Ocho Rios and he told me he had looked up the "footprints" story and he had a dream about Jesus carrying him. I told him Jesus wanted him to be His and was giving him the opportunity to come to Him. He said he thought he was called to be a preacher. He didn't have much time to talk, so I told him to pray to Jesus as soon as he could.

I decided to spend the afternoon at the resort, so I found a comfortable lounge chair on the beach. I noticed a man who kept walking past me, staring. He walked farther up the beach, but then stopped, turned around, and walked straight back to me. He excused himself for the interruption, but explained he had seen this bright light all around me and was curious about it. When he decided to ignore it and continue walking up the beach, he said a voice told him to go back to the lady with the bright light, and she would tell him what to do. I explained to Him the Light was Jesus and He wanted him to accept Him as the Savior and Lord of his life. I talked to him about salvation in Jesus, and he prayed to receive Him. Immediately, he broke out in a song of praise and worship to the Lord. He started shaking and crying. It was breathtaking and beautiful. When he finished, he said he didn't know where that came from and nothing like that had ever happened to him before. I told him Jesus gave him the gift of music and He would use his gift to preach the gospel. He was so excited he thanked me and ran up the beach to tell his friends.

Vendors walked up and down the beach selling their trinkets. I talked with most of them about Jesus. It saddened me to hear repeated stories showing no interest in Jesus because many people in churches, who also talked about Jesus, hurt them and were not very kind to them. I responded by telling them I was not there to talk about churches or the people in them. I was there to talk about the real Jesus who loved them and gave His life for them. They listened but were cautious.

One girl brought towels to my room. I asked how she was doing, and she broke down and cried. She told me about the physical abuse she receives from her husband. She expressed concern for her daughters having to be around him. We prayed and asked God to help her, heal her wounds, deliver her and her daughters from the situation, deal with her husband and save him, and fill her with His peace and joy.

Thursday was Valentine's Day. It was difficult for me because only a year before I spent the day with Ken on what was to be our last "date" together. It was a beautiful day, so I drove to a nearby beach. Along the way, I stopped at a stand where artisans sold their wood carvings. The pieces were gorgeous, and I bought a few of them for gifts. I then asked if they knew Jesus. One man replied, "Who is Jesus? I don't see Jesus. Where is He? How can He be real if you can't see Him?" He crossed his arms and appeared to be testing me. I explained the gift of salvation Jesus offered them and told them He had a plan for their lives. I asked if they wanted me to pray for them. The obstinate man continued to fold his arms in defiance, but an older man walked up from the back of the group, looked at them, and told them to "bow your heads, close your eyes, and pray." The other man continued to keep his arms folded, but the older man repeated himself, and then he obeyed. *"It worked."* So I prayed Jesus would reveal Himself to them in a mighty way, and they would know the plan God had for each one of them. They thanked me and told me they would watch for me when I drove past to go back to the resort.

I decided to do something fun, so I went parasailing for the first time in my life. This was an unusual experience for me, because I used to be afraid of heights until God delivered me from it, and to do it by myself was even more humorous. I admit, however, it was quite exciting. I was the first one up, so the captain gave me a long ride and let me drift high above the beach. The view was breathtaking.

As I drove back to the resort, the woodcarvers were true to their word and waved for me to stop. When I walked up to their stand, the older man told me Jesus had visited them after I prayed and their day with Him was wonderful. He then presented me with a hand-carved walking stick he had made. He said, "Now you can take this around the world when you tell people about Jesus!" I was shocked because I never mentioned any such thing to them. It truly blessed me. I wondered as I left what plan God had in store for me, especially after what the older man said.

When I returned to the resort, a young girl met me in front and said everyone was talking about the preacher lady and how she prayed for everyone.

She said many of their lives had been changed and God truly sent me there. I explained she needed to tell them it was really only Jesus—I was only the messenger, but He is the Savior and Lord of all of our lives. She agreed.

The following morning, as I was about to exit the resort for a day of sightseeing, the security woman stopped me and had me park the car. As I approached her, she asked if I was the Christian lady everyone was talking about. I told her I was a Christian who belonged to Jesus. "Yes, you are the one," she stated. She proceeded to tell me about her 15-year-old daughter who was almost blind from an eye disease. She said she had a dream the night before and an angel in the dream told her to find the Christian lady and have her pray. I asked her first if she belonged to Jesus, and she said "no." I explained it would begin with her first because we couldn't agree together that Jesus would heal her daughter unless she knew Him as the Savior of her life. She prayed and began to cry. Then we prayed for Jesus the Healer to touch her daughter's eyes and heal her. I felt the power of God go straight through me and into the woman. She almost fell to the ground. (I guess I should have warned her about that!) By then, the woman was weeping, so I knew I needed to leave because she was working, and I didn't want to get her into trouble. I told her I would stop by and see her when I returned.

Upon returning several hours later, she stopped me again and excitedly told me she had called her daughter at school. Her daughter said "someone" had touched her (although there was no one around), the tearing had stopped, and she could see clearly. *"Praise the Lord."* We hugged, praised Jesus, and danced in the parking lot. We were so blessed to see what the Lord had done for her precious daughter.

One young man came up to me and said, "You are not like the people in churches, but like someone who cares, sent by Jesus!" I always try to reinforce the fact that Jesus is the One to be thanked and praised.

One of the vendors from the beach found me to offer a cross he made for me. It was the only cross I had seen anyone carry on the beach. It was a simple, wooden cross, but it meant the world because he made it just for me. I asked him to carve his name in the back so I could remember him and pray for him. He told me he wanted to make sure I had it before I returned to the United States. What an incredible man!

On Saturday, all of the vendors were looking for me, trying to give me small tokens of their friendship. Some of them finally wanted me to pray with them. One of the women especially wanted to find me because she had something to tell me. She looked me in the eyes and told me all the vendors talked it over, and they all agreed the preacher lady "was the real deal—not fake!" Then she asked me to pray for her and her daughter.

As I walked around the resort, I met a woman and her daughter selling jewelry by the pool. The woman asked me to speak to her daughter who had bitterness in her heart towards her father. She said she had not smiled in years. I talked to her about the love her heavenly Father had for her, and bitterness only put her in a box, while her biological father was still free to do what he wanted to do. I told her Jesus, being nailed to the cross, looked down at his accusers and said, "Father, forgive them for they know not what they do." She needed to realize the love of Jesus reaches down into the inner most part of our being to set us free from the hurts others inflict upon us. She wanted to pray, so we asked Jesus to deliver her and asked that she would be able to forgive her father. When we finished, she smiled, and her mother cried for joy.

Throughout the day, employees came and found me one by one. Some presented their names and addresses, others wanted prayer, some were crying, and many just wanted to give me a hug. I was so overwhelmed with what God had done. I didn't want to leave either, and wished I could stay another week or longer.

I cried too, wondering who would help these Jamaican people to know Jesus. Many of them didn't have Bibles. There were many needs, both spiritual and physical, so I prayed God would send laborers into the harvest because the harvest is truly great but the laborers are few in number. I also prayed He would send me back to Jamaica.

This trip would not have been possible except Christians back home and around the world were praying for God to touch this little country. I reached as many as possible with the gospel, but seeds had been sown by others as well. We have all worked together to advance the Kingdom of God in what-ever capacity we were called. Sometimes, though, it seems like it's still not enough.

Sunday, I spent my last hours at the resort going to breakfast and talking with the employees I had not seen previously. One girl behind the bar gave me coffee. I asked her if she knew Jesus. She said she didn't. Although she was working, I did have a few minutes to tell her about Jesus who died for her. I explained she could pray and ask Him into her heart even while she was working. I asked her to consider Him and to remember what I told her because Jesus had a plan for her life. She asked me to pray for her and not forget her.

An older man who knew about "the preacher lady" sang a song, based on Psalm 100, while I drank my coffee. He said he wanted to sing for the Lord all around the world. I believe he will. He had such a love for Jesus.

An elderly employee who tended all the landscaping asked me to take his picture. He did such a nice job tending the grounds. He stood there, tall, with a grin on his face, ready to be photographed. Then he asked me to please send it to him.

My next stop was back to the airport in Montego Bay. My journey was over, and it was time to return home. As I watched the island disappear, I prayed for all those I left behind. I prayed God would send me back. I prayed for laborers in the harvest. I knew my body got back on that airplane, but my heart stayed in Jamaica.

Since I have been home, I have spoken to many people about what God did in Jamaica. Most people thought it was fascinating. Some people were skeptical, thinking it could never happen that way in this day and age. What matters most to me is that Jesus is glorified in all things. He is the One who will make a difference in the lives of all those who believe!

CHAPTER 15

FOR YOU

This chapter, the final one, is dedicated to you, the reader. For you see, this is not the end of the book, merely the beginning. All the stories recorded in this book are true. They are mine; I own them. However, God wants to do exceptional things in your life as well. He wants you to expect great things from Him because He is the Almighty God, Creator and Ruler of all things. He has a plan for your life that far surpasses anything you have experienced so far. You were made for His purpose, for His glory, for His love.

Several years ago, I became interested in knowing about diamonds, particularly since I found one. Aside from their significant beauty and worth, I thought there must be a spiritual significance associated with them. So, I read several articles and found that a diamond is created by intense heat and pressure. You can only cut a diamond with another diamond. We are being formed into diamonds of great worth to the Master. Sometimes great trials and tribulations come upon us to shape and form us. Sometimes we have to be cut and polished to bring out our true beauty in the Lord. In every way, we are being molded into His image. It doesn't come through the easy times. It comes through the trying times.

People may not see your beauty from within. They may criticize you, condemn you, and even give up on you, but Jesus never gives up. He has a plan for your life and wants you to know of His everlasting love for you. He is your refuge. He is your hope.

For those of you who belong to Him, I encourage you to get closer, go farther, trust Him more, get out of your comfort zones, stretch your faith, and believe Him for awesome things. Put away the things distracting you from spending precious time in His presence and in His Word. Don't be satisfied with what you have experienced up until now. There is so much more of Him that He wants you to know and experience. Launch out into the deep waters. Don't miss what He created you for!

If you do not know Jesus as your Savior and Lord, He wants you to come to Him just as you are. You are special and important to Him, and He loves you more than you know. He extends to you forgiveness and a new life in Him. He makes you a brand new person. Second Corinthians 5:17 says it this way, "Therefore, if anyone is in Christ, he is a new creation; old things have passed away, behold, all things have become new." It only takes a simple prayer from your heart: Jesus, I need You. I believe You are the Son of God who came and died on a cross for my sins. Please forgive me of all I have done wrong. I ask that You come into my life and heart and be my Lord today and forever. I surrender my life to You so Your life will come forth in me. Thank You that I am now a new creation in You. Help me to be all that You created me to be for Your glory. I pray in Jesus name, Amen.

You will never be the same as you embark on this spiritual journey with the Savior!

Will you trust Him?

Printed in the United States
204854BV00001B/160-288/P